Gathering Broken Light

Heather Lang-Cassera

For information contact:
Unsolicited Press
Portland, Oregon
www.unsolicitedpress.com
orders@unsolicitedpress.com
619-354-8005

Cover Design: Kathryn Gerhardt
Editor: S.R. Stewart

ISBN: 978-1-950730-92-6

In memory and in honor
of the victims and survivors of 1 October

The tension above
the water glass

foreshadows the moon
just this once.

The mourning dove
brushes the sill like

a finger on a
trigger.

The prickly pear flickers
silent in the late heat, with flame
-like petals,

snapshots of a moment,
supergiant stars,
as the sky has fallen & settles

to the coral-red floor of our still-raw earth.

Some things are meant to be seen, not touched,
never heard,

& so we wait, confronting
pasts we cannot understand, futures
that can only

be wrongly predicted.

Nopales wave us forward, gestures
of kindness when least
expected,

juxtaposed against the mountains, torn
against deep blue
& those that came before.

Even this desert was once an ocean.

In an alphabet of grief—

arching bonfires carried destruction

each feather gasped

hills inverted

just knowing love made night open

pushing quiet resolutions

stars tasted

unfractured...

The abandoned napkin is a collapsed cloud.

Which is to say we leave it behind.

The sky has fallen
& we cannot take it with us.

The night exhaled, its lungs sunken to absence,
misshapen rooms light cannot enter.

What might we whet with mothers' tongues

to clean the paper-thin skin
of messy babes' mouths, while ring fingers capture
tears, trace faces.

Who in the Mojave has not caught drops
of rainwater on the beds

that live beneath the roofs of our mouths,

empty chambers
which hold our breaths.

The abandoned
napkin is a collapsed cloud,

a prayer that we can see, until it isn't,
a thought we hope
to decipher before snuffed out.

A small breath billows
before it fades.

Beaks of birds emerge
from crumpled paper,

concrete nouns shimmering against
what we might pretend
to see as a winter landscape,

a failed anticipation of something new.

Through proximity, what else
have we forgotten?

We wait, the shape of this
small home, with roof more gentle
than steeple, tugging us

toward the ground,
asking

us about the last
time that we felt something, truly.

Beneath a gathering of leaves
(by whom? we do not know)
we find a tear-stained something.

This something in the leaves
(in the heart of the woods? who are we to decide)
finds itself

shifted back & forth by the ground squirrel with
paws so delicate
they might hurt,

or by the sharp heaviness
of hooves, those of bighorn sheep, but never

by the clear wind which
cannot gain strength beyond the gentleness
of a breeze, here,

in the dead of the joyful night
(married, for now, to this, a phrase so
misunderstood).

Oh, to be

something that is undefined, to be something

that is yet to be.

I walk toward the hills
& cannot remember your name.

You warned me,
in the night, I would forget the deepest
angles, the sleep-swept octaves of your voice.

What else have I capsized?

I dogear pages to temper swollen verbs,
phrases posing without shadow,
moving forward without doubt,

our shared words now lifted, like pollen, skyward
becoming the stars.

You deserve to be remembered.

How can I keep
hope-drenched moments
between curled hands—

In this moonlight, a pause, a
perspective, we become
something better & something less.

This grief returning. Again & again.

You could say we were hopeful.

I don't know.

I see the slow moonlight
as something we cannot avoid,
something to which we can only surrender

like the claw-footed
bathtub of our first home
with feet furling & unfurling & both at once—

Who can say.

Enamored with small
things, I believed that dream was real for the first
too-many-hours of the new day.

Your hands are empty canyons
that cannot hold
your fight-or-flight heart no matter your efforts,

so, instead, you press your remade house
key to a topography

that we will never understand.

We contemplate
the listlessness

which we find both in love & in loss.

I wish I could sing the sky to you.

I dream of holding

her small & curled hand
up to the sky

of learning that even her delicate fist

could have eclipsed
the center of our solar system,

even though this is only
because we are so far away.

We are such machines
preparing to respond
until we vanish.

Maybe waiting is all that we have

& maybe
there is solace in knowing
that even the sun launches flares,

which take time to reach us.

I cannot help but wonder
which never-learned lullabies
could have best passed

each of those nine minutes.

In an alphabet of grief—

a buildable city

dipped endlessly

fireflies gave heed

illuminated jars kept lonely

marigolds nodded overlooking pasts

quietly resisting stoicism

trembling unstoppable…

A trampled cup is a deserted snow globe.

It snows in this southern valley
once a year, maybe,
a sprinkling.

A friend writes about unexpected snow
like spilled flakes of mashed potatoes,
a food too warm, too
comforting for summer, spring,

& now fall.

We are grateful
the snow is not rain,
that the weather anchor does not predict *showers*,

a word that reminds us of bullets.

A trampled cup reminds us of a snow globe
which reminds us of dreaming
of a white christmas,

one before the summoning of ghosts,
one before the faces washed pale by floodlights,
one before the eyes wider than the mouths
of *oh, holy night.*

These plastic edges look sharper than they are,
but perception's foundation is memory
&, yes, we remember.

A turn of favorite paperback page
reminds us of loss, a delicate

papercut carving
a hidden crescent moon,
or a passage

to the needless harvesting of hearts.

Of this trampled cup, desert sand
has been swept inside, looking as if, instead,
it is spilling out, extending itself

across *all the ends of the earth,*
which is to say, yes,
we see the Mojave in your once-hazel eyes.

We have never owned
a snow globe, never kept one on a shelf like a secret story
to be told again & again

& we will never wonder what it might be like
to hold something

in the palms of one's own hands, to shake an
entire world

while the stillness of the scene
remains untouched,

a narrative merely implied.

To weave the sky
completely over, the moment leaps

in all
    directions.

My mouth holds space for these lost words
as if a creature, tender
as the darkness,

might someday rest on the stillness of my tongue

here, in this body where
our pale wrists have been underbellies
bathing in everything we have ever done
& undone.

The hills behind our home are still.
We watch them

& we feel
the snow-throbbing heart & the birch-white
spines

that sing from sharp, gentle spaces.

Inside, we find galaxies
within handfuls of carefully
halved grapes which we eat, piece by piece,

just before midnight
remembering, also, the unknown tracks
we followed at dusk,

the ones we tried not to cover with our own.

Tonight, we wish for another small snowfall,
one that will allow us
to have,

both new & again, what we held today,
surrounding us, tomorrow.

These lengthening
days have knit mittens with holes

beneath the softest spaces

as if something somewhere believed
that we could open ourselves,

could touch the clouds with our own bare offerings,

could lead a dove to know
she does not need

to fly away during wintertime,
to understand that her sweet, strong

song could, with patience, melt through
the deep

forgiveness of snow.

A faint voice, a strange request,

& nothing—
a death-glimmer of sea birds

hiding below
the surface,
            lost.

Forget the humming,
the middle battle, the pipe

in mouth.

A row of steady oars
attacks the trusted
shadows.

A rope begins to cut
the water.

Teeth, nimble, climb
then lower

a joyful shout.
Surrounded by sound,

this spare figure twists

until the whispers
perched & pulled our backs
like toothpicks,

a struggle to howl
like dry matches.

In a frantic nine-minute window of intermittent gunfire
the barrels can reach several hundred degrees.
Components used together in a weapon suggest a desire

to shoot large amounts of automatic-like fire,
turning orange & even blue as rounds travel thousands
      of feet,
in a frantic nine-minute window of intermittent gunfire.

Nevada Law allows the purchase of machine guns
      & silencers,
a meticulous collection of accessories.
Components used together in a weapon suggest a desire.

An AR-15 type rifle with a bump or slide fire
(automatic weapons used by the military have lever releases)
in a frantic nine-minute window of intermittent gunfire

bounce, or bump, the weapon into the trigger finger.
The bump fire mechanism includes a high capacity.
Components used together in a weapon suggest a desire,

which helps the shooter acquire...
Regulate the size of high-capacity magazines.
In a frantic nine-minute window of intermittent gunfire
components used together in a weapon suggest a desire.

Lanterns, aching,
continue to circle,

fight for a place, drift
to the following
day.

Wind-blown corners
of rough voices ask

so many questions.

Desert fossils
shout
        without a word.

We hear nothing

but repeated facts
carried by efforts

turned.

In an alphabet of grief—

a blank cocoon divides eternity

falcons gather

hurricanes ignite

jump-starting kinetics

limitless magnolias nod off

predators quiet rebellious silences

time unravels...

Through rapture come undone,

we sift through failing points of view.
The sand breathes beneath the sky, respirations

of sunlight,
as if settling

like snow to the earth.

There was a season
of saying
   yes.

The aluminum can is a failing telescope,

which is to say
we cannot go back.

We see even Mars
as it was twelve minutes ago,

another red-rocked place
where we have gone in search of water.

There are so many metaphors for oceans
& for loss.

The city lights whisper washes,
disguise the sky,
slip man-made canopies

over us, pretending
to shelter us.

The aluminum can is a failed
telescope, one never tilted up

& into this late-night sky.

I called my mother's dry voice desert
years before I knew the beauty
of the Mojave. Perhaps
this was patience. Maybe
this was becoming.
Here, staccato
cacti wait. I
beg,
    sing.

Life must come to the surface.

The hammer tapping
across the gray
fog brightly.

Salt-cracked faces,
humming to the fire.

The morning borrows the land behind us.

Gathering broken
light, we no longer drift
over the sun.

In an alphabet of grief—

a baby coyote drinks eloquently

fiery gills hum

into jeweled knives like

magnificent never-ending

omniscient puddles quietly rambling

stubborn tumbleweeds

overturn...

The desert tortoise makes her way,
not as if she could move mountains;
she is the buttes & saddlebacks

& is too perfect to be a fixed part
of this dust-splashed earth.

She swishes sand, leaving wing-shaped tracks,

& on her back, carries a detailed
topographic map:

the delicate lines, contours of relief,
or manifestation of the gaps

we fill with silence & other absent declarations.

Together, we hear the hearty hissing
& guttural grunts, warning

us to keep our distance.
We thought the tortoise was a snake,
but we learn

even our palms,
such unquiet basins

can ache.

The marks the firearm leaves
on its projectile:

ballistic fingerprints.

After dark, you show me
the stone structures of Rhyolite,

built long before the fire.

Your hands discover
their own

alphabet amongst my ribs,
guided only

by sound.

Can we talk about the clouds? you ask.
In the sky, salmon meets fire

orange against cyan blue,
leaving small saguaro

silhouettes, empty
hands, or shadow

puppets of
cold, toy

guns.

A slender statue
has become the night—

flashing restless anger
deeper

into what?
We do not agree.

They came like shattered
rain. They came

like unstoppable mouths,

already closed,
like unnatural divers

without hands pressed together,

nothing like prayer, moving so quickly
country plains
became mountains

that could chew up this desert sky.

I say this
because I was not there.
I am told

those bullets were like nothing else,
these metaphors attempts to dissociate

or to try to understand,
but nothing in between.

I promise to listen to you
speak in whichever love language you choose
& to know that this

will never be enough
because sometimes, still,

we hold our breaths

as if we are
under water.

We trespass

to find that blue diamond cholla,

when backlit, are breathtaking
with small haloes

behind savior-like spines.

Though rare, once found,
they brim in numbers.

We drive east just far enough
to be one time zone farther.

We stop for fuel
& wade through

some sort of white light.

We paw at cans
of Campbell's soup,

a water gun,
a box of Tylenol,
& a superhero

Kleenex box.
We become today's
postmodern desert outlaws

a strange vying
I would never wish on anyone.

We are silently drowning one moment at a time,

& it is always
to that same

goddamn that's-not-love song,

which leaves me wondering
what is set to repeat,

but oh honey, yes,
there is water, still, here
in the Mojave.

In an alphabet of grief—

a brief chaos digs endlessly

flamingos glisten halfheartedly

intricate journeys

kept landlocked

maps never opened

papas quiet restless sons

tsunamis unhinge...

A prayer to the late Mars rover, Opportunity—

like us, you were
solar powered, & you, too, found water

where we thought none might be.

They say you were lost
during the worst storm
recorded in Mars' history,

that our final calls to wake you
have gone unanswered.

They say that you, too, witnessed
dust devils, & you photographed your tracks
in the sand, & for you, Oppy,

a true god from the machine,
who lived fifty-five times your projected lifespan,

we mourn.

Because of your humanity, we cannot
help but recall the concert goers lost
during the harvest festival,

the storm of bullets on our own
red-rocked planet.

Maybe, someday, the sites of October 1
& Sol 5111 will become
the first interstellar places, sister cities,
to belong together.

We think of the victims & of the survivors
& dream of how
they danced & held hands.

We ask, on Mars,
did you & your twin, Spirit, play earth
schoolyard games?

Send us back over
        our fifty-eight souls lost
on the first of October...

Our *deus ex machina,*
our Red Rover, please forgive us

as we beg.

There is something about a cactus that appears as a star
only from its aerial view,

& as a globe only when young &
then with wooly contrails that appear with age
beneath thousands of cyan-blue skies whispering,

somehow, all of the seasons' names at once.

Its ribs twisted after some years,
& now I think of your floating rib,
which will never be quite right

because you didn't mean it when you promised
you would rest & let it heal.

The doctor explained there are both true
& false ribs,

which might have been when you stopped listening.

Today, when you turn,
like the astrophytum we planted so many years ago,
& you gasp

because something is now
where it should not be,

I cannot help but think of the barely rooted cactus,
of our decades-old home, of the narratives
we are built to create

in these imperfect vessels.

Humming as quietly as sunfall,
obeying the curvature of the earth,
mending memories by creating new ones,
every day we wake up,
morning arriving too soon,
except that we still have each other—
arrhythmias of soft, but seismic, affection,
needle & thread played by a cloud unraveling,
silently tugging at our thoughts,
not acknowledging our pasts despite
earthquakes' shivering aftershocks,
vulnerable midnight chats
about almost nothing—
do you love me as when we first met?
Here, even arches open with the friction
of wind & time.

Luxury is the blue
scorpion, something
like the sky

with shell segmented

like wind-chapped
knuckles.

You tell me about the excitement of igniting
a tumbleweed,

& I think of a cage turned outward, protecting
empty space within.

I contemplate what we should do
in a controlled environment only,
or not at all.

Bring me all of your worst ideas.
What I mean is

let's roll them all across this once-ocean floor,

beneath the clouded ripples
of our sea-less sky
& away.

At night, the desert dusts itself off,
& century plants continue to bloom

slowly, like stars burn.
How can we learn to abandon what has already left us?

We keep secrets so well
while the desert heat sinks unknowingly

through us.

Monsoon season
calls for us to drop everything,
to listen to the thunder,

a shattering sound too low to be any bone-china plate.

Looking out, you call me
honey locust, firecracker,
tranquil pond,

names stolen

from paint swatches
as if this is how you might find

the next version of me
you could live with.

The lightning outside
looks like skeletons that have fallen
out of our closets,

& buried themselves &
then grown in their own unpredictable ways

like vessels that have been capsized but never captured.

I hope the power goes out,
but it does not.

I ask you to describe the rain,
but you do not.

You also talk a little too loudly,
but I remind myself
that someday

I could miss this.

A white feather floats
something like surrender

on top of your sparkling water,
still resting, between you & me.

I look too closely
at the feather's fine lines
& wonder if you, too,

are reading between them.

Everyone knows about the hollow portion
of an avian mast, the quill,

which once allowed us to write, with our own hands,

love letters as light and real
as birdsong,

but I wonder if you know
the true anatomy,

that there are barbs
& that there are many &
that they are considered, by some,

to be feathers within the feather.
Have you, too, looked closely at this
petite & elegant lifeboat,

suspended between us,
beneath the desert sun
& above too many cubes of ice.

The afterfeather,
this unkempt underbelly
of perfect plume,

can only give comfort,
was never expected to be able to push

anyone's chambered heart into flight.

There is a plurality
to mammals.

Your breath becomes
a giraffe rising from a nothingness,

beautiful & strange

with incredible heart. Glances are exchanged,
light like sheets of paper
slipping from the air,

forgotten, too soon, beneath bare feet.

Let's build fire
with the oars of yesterday's
boats

near rivers of tall grasses.

Tell me why
these wrists fail

to remember, having whispered
but never having known enough.

Grief blooms even
from the topography
of small rocks.

We wait for what
we cannot understand,
wonder what life might be like

if our own herd were called
a tower.

Your hand, a basin lifted up
from this earth, brought
skyward and emptied
of rivers, of pond, of gravity
for this, a quiet kind of love—
promise me you will go on,
feel the percussion of tears,
the moon as emptiness traced
and brimming with promise,
because both can be true,
with dreams being antlers
we shed with whims outside
of our control, with the fox's tufts
of hair being silky pairs of beds
within hungry, prayer-like ears,
distant and open for broken
ideas once gorgeous.

With the darkening of honeyed blue
above, I sit on the roof of our new home
in the humming of the air conditioner,

a lullaby, reimagined.

Downstairs, our dog yawns. Her crooked teeth
are like the night sky, predictable by memory

& according to absence.

A distant air
nears my spine,

a sinking ship,

the rusted bones & teeth
of empty beds
that are too cold

to argue.

We said that we
would

try.

I have never known loss
like longing.

I took words & placed them on my tongue,
a quiet catapult for what
I cannot say.

I think of your wrists,
but as city swans in pairs
dark with moonlight.

And your ribcage,
undiscoverable.

Here, I wait
with ceramic bowl, clean & grey as shadow,
between two hands
so that I might feel

the something that is in emptiness.

What are we
without certainty,
but the trees without hills are no less
for their loneliness.

And these promises, rearranged—
a wing unbroken, a softness
not surrendered.

INDEX OF FIRST LINES (IN ORDER OF APPEARANCE)

ACKNOWLEDGEMENTS

Versions of these poems first appeared in *Architrave*; *The Del Sol Review*; *diode*; *HOOT*; *I was the girl with the moon-shaped face* (Zeitgeist Press); *Lady/Liberty/Lit*; *Lumina*; *The Meadow*; Nevada Humanities' *Double Down* blog; the Nevada Humanities *Margaret, Are You Grieving* exhibition; Nevada Public Radio's *Desert Companion* blog; *North American Review*; *Sandstone & Silver: An Anthology of Nevada Poets* (Zeitgeist Press); *South Dakota Review*; *Whiskey Island*; and *Witness'* blog.

The poems with the following first lines were written after photographer David Becker's "Reported Shooting at Mandalay Bay in Las Vegas" photographs for *Getty Images News*: "The abandoned napkin is a collapsed cloud," "The aluminum can is a failing telescope," and "A trampled cup is a deserted snow globe."

The poem which begins with "In a frantic nine-minute window of intermittent gunfire" is composed of lines from an article in *The Washington Post* by Alex Horton, "The Las Vegas shooter modified a dozen rifles to shoot like automatic weapons."

The poem with the first line "A prayer to the late Mars rover, Opportunity—" is in conversation with an article from *Salon* by Nicole Karlis, "A grieving Earth says goodbye to Martian rover Opportunity: Ironically, it took a robot's death to bring together humanity."

Through a Project Grant for Artists, the writing of this book was supported, in part, by the Nevada Arts Council, a state agency, which receives support from the National Endowment for the Arts, a federal agency, and the state of Nevada.

About the Author

Heather Lang-Cassera lives in Las Vegas, Nevada where she served as Clark County Poet Laureate (2019-2021) and was named 2017 "Best Local Writer or Poet" by the readers of Nevada Public Radio's *Desert Companion*. Heather holds a Master of Fine Arts in Creative Writing from Fairleigh Dickinson University with a Graduate Certificate in Literary Translation. She is a founder of and the Senior Editor for Tolsun Books, a Faculty Advisor for *300 Days of Sun*, and the World Literature Editor and a literary critic for *The Literary Review*. Her chapbook, *I was the girl with the moon-shaped face*, was published by Zeitgeist Press. At Nevada State College, Heather teaches College Success, Composition, Creative Writing, and Literature.

Learn more at www.heatherlang.cassera.net